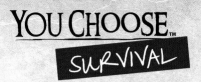

YOU CHOOSE™
SURVIVAL

Can You Survive
THE
DESERT?

An Interactive Survival Adventure

D0878940

by Matt Doeden

Consultant:
Marjorie "Slim" Woodruff, PhD
Instructor, Grand Canyon Field Institute

CAPSTONE PRESS
a capstone imprint

You Choose Books are published by Capstone Press,
1710 Roe Crest Drive, North Mankato, Minnesota 56003.
www.capstonepub.com

Books published by Capstone Press are manufactured with paper
containing at least 10 percent post-consumer waste.

Library of Congress Cataloging-in-Publication Data
Doeden, Matt.
Can you survive the desert? : an interactive survival adventure / by Matt Doeden.
    p. cm. — (You choose. Survival)
 Summary: "Describes the fight for survival while exploring the Sahara, Sonoran, and
Gobi Deserts"—Provided by publisher.
 Includes bibliographical references and index.
 ISBN 978-1-4296-7543-7 (library binding)
 ISBN 978-1-4296-7995-4 (paperback)
1. Desert survival—Juvenile literature. I. Title. II. Series.
 GV200.5.D63 2012
 613.6909154—dc22   2011035741

Editorial Credits
Angie Kaelberer, editor; Gene Bentdahl, designer; Eric Gohl, media researcher;
   Laura Manthe, production specialist

Photo Credits
Alamy/imagebroker, 90; Alamy/mediacolor's, 104; Alamy/Tom Uhlman, 38; Ardea/
Steve Downer, 25; Capstone Studio/Karon Dubke, cover (front); Corbis/Danny
Lehman, 12; Corbis/Yann Arthus-Bertrand, 16; Getty Images/National Geographic/
James P. Blair, 40; Getty Images/Per-Anders Pettersson, 72; Getty Images/Simon
Weller, 98; Getty Images/The Image Bank/Nivek Neslo, 67; Newscom/Photoshot/
Xinhua/Zhang Honkxiang, 86; Newscom/ZUMA Press/l75, 81; Photo Researchers,
Inc/Dan Suzio, 47; Shutterstock/Christa DeRidder, 30; Shutterstock/evantravels, 54;
Shutterstock/Galyna Andrushko, 10, 70; Shutterstock/Gary Yim, 36; Shutterstock/
Jason Swarr, 44; Shutterstock/Kanwarjit Singh Boparai, 61; Shutterstock/Pascal
RATEAU, 74; Shutterstock/Pichugin Dmitry, 95; Shutterstock/Sebastien Burel, 102;
Shutterstock/Steve Bower, 65; Shutterstock/Steve Byland, 57; Shutterstock/Vladimir
Melnik, 34; Shutterstock/Vladimir Wrangel, 100; Shutterstock/Wilson Chan, 6;
Shutterstock/Yarik, 69; Shutterstock/Yellowj, cover (back)

Printed in the United States of America in Stevens Point, Wisconsin.
022013   007177R

TABLE OF CONTENTS

About Your
ADVENTURE

You are lost in the desert, one of the most dangerous places on Earth. Water is almost impossible to find. The daytime sun bakes you with intense heat. The nights can be brutally cold. Venomous snakes and scorpions lurk under rocks.

In this book you'll deal with extreme survival situations. You'll explore how the knowledge you have and the choices you make can mean the difference between life and death. Chapter One sets the scene. Then you choose which path to read. Follow the directions at the bottom of each page. The choices you make will change your outcome. After you finish one path, go back and read the others for new perspectives and more adventures.

YOU CHOOSE the path you
take through your adventure.

Desert plants need little water to survive.

welcome to the Desert

You're in the desert, one of the least welcoming places on Earth. Water and food are scarce. Temperatures swing wildly from extreme heat to bitter cold. Venomous snakes, scorpions, and spiders lurk in the sand's cracks and crevices.

Deserts cover about 20 percent of Earth's land area. But they're not all hot. Scientists define a desert as any area that receives an average of less than 10 inches of precipitation per year. Because of this fact, the cold continent of Antarctica is considered a desert.

Turn the page.

North
America

Asia

Europe

Sonoran
Desert

N
W   E
S

Sahara
Desert

Africa

Desert

South
America

Gobi
Desert

0   1000   2000 Km
0   500   1000 Mile

Australia

Antarctica

With so little moisture, deserts can't support
much plant and animal life. Only life adapted to
such harsh conditions can live there.

Deserts are the result of weather patterns. One of the most common is a rain shadow. Rain shadows often form near a large mountain range. Air flows over the mountains. It cools as it rises. As the air cools, its moisture falls on the mountains as rain or snow. On the far side of the mountains, the dry air brings little rain. The area in this rain shadow becomes a desert.

Every continent has deserts. In North America the Mojave and Sonoran cover parts of Mexico and the southwestern United States. Northern Africa is home to the vast Sahara. The Kalahari lies in southern Africa. The huge Gobi desert stretches across Asia, while central Australia holds the Australian Desert. And these are just a few.

Turn the page.

The desert can be a brutal place even for a prepared traveler.

You'll have to figure out how to survive in such a harsh environment. How will you find water and food? Can you avoid deadly wildlife? How can you find your way to civilization and safety? It won't be easy. Are you ready for the challenge?

To take your chances in Africa's Sahara, turn to page 13.

To test your survival skills in North America's Sonoran Desert, turn to page 39.

To see if you have what it takes to survive Asia's Gobi, turn to page 71.

Help can take a long time to reach a desert plane wreck.

CHAPTER 2

Surviving the Sahara

You're half asleep as you gaze out the window of the airplane. Below you lies mile after mile of sand dunes and rocky desert floor.

You're one of just four passengers on the small airplane. It's taking you north toward Cairo, Egypt. There you'll board a jet taking you back home. You've spent two months teaching English to students in small African villages, but now your trip is over. You're eager to return to the comforts of home.

Just as you drift off to sleep, a violent shaking awakens you. The lights in the plane's cabin flicker and die. The plane is dropping rapidly. Something is wrong! Behind you, an elderly woman screams.

Turn the page.

The dull roar of the engines falls silent. With a chill you realize that the plane is going down. You try to take deep breaths. Others in the cabin are panicking. Some are trying to get out of their seats. You check that your seat belt is secure, and then grab the backpack stuffed under the seat.

You remember nothing of the impact. You lose consciousness as soon as the plane hits the ground.

Sometime later you open your eyes. You're groggy, and your forehead is bleeding. A warm, dry wind blows against your face. You're alive! But the good news ends there. The plane ripped into two pieces. You unbuckle and check for other survivors. Everyone else is dead, including the pilot. You are alone and lost in the Sahara Desert.

The plane was small and privately owned. You're not sure if the pilot filed a flight plan. It's unlikely that anyone even knows you're out here.

To stay with the wreckage, turn to page **16.**

To gather supplies and search for safety, turn to page **18.**

Sand and wind can quickly bury wreckage in the desert.

There's no way you're going to wander off into the Sahara in the middle of the day. The plane's wreckage will provide shelter. Eventually someone will realize the plane is missing and come searching. This is the best place to be found.

In what's left of the cockpit, you find two bottles of water, two bags of potato chips, and a book of matches. You also grab a seat cushion. You gather everything and head outside. You'll use the plane's shadow as shelter. Staying inside with the dead bodies just isn't an option.

The sun dips as evening comes. The air rapidly starts to cool. You build a small fire, using some of the dry brush that grows here as well the stuffing from the seat cushion.

At dawn you have a decision to make. You're down to a little more than one bottle of water. If you're going to move, it has to be now.

To stay where you are, turn to page **20**.

To head in the direction of the lights, turn to page **21**.

In what's left of the cockpit, you find two bottles of water and two bags of potato chips. You stuff them into your backpack and head out toward a stand of rocky hills in the distance.

It's late afternoon, and the sun is brutally hot. You dig your baseball cap and a T-shirt out of your pack. You wrap the shirt around your face. Breathing through the cloth will help your body save moisture.

After just 30 minutes, you're already drenched in sweat. Moving over the desert's sand and rock is hard work. You drink from one of the water bottles. You know you will become dehydrated quickly.

Finally you reach the steep, rocky hills. They look difficult to climb. You could keep walking along them, looking for an easier route. But you're eager to climb as high as you can. You hope to see some sign of people.

To search for a safer climbing spot, turn to page **21**.

To climb here, turn to page **24**.

You can survive here for a few days. You're sure someone will find you by then. You spend the morning going through the wreckage, looking for more supplies. You don't find much. Soon your water is gone. Even in the shade, it's incredibly hot. You're sweating and losing precious moisture every time you move.

Late in the afternoon, you have to empty your bladder. You know that urine is mostly water. You can capture it in your empty water bottle and drink it. But urine is also very salty. Just the thought of drinking it makes you sick. You're not sure you're that desperate. Not yet, anyway.

To capture and drink your own urine, turn to page **28.**

To not risk drinking the urine, turn to page **30.**

You need to get to high ground, but you're not willing to risk a fall that could kill you. You keep walking along the ridge. Half an hour later, you find a much better spot for climbing, with a gentler slope and sturdier rock.

Carefully you scale the rock. You move slowly, taking your time. You examine every handhold and foothold. Snakes and scorpions often make their homes under rocks.

By the time you reach the top, the sun is starting to set. You gather some desert brush and build a small fire. You'll sleep here tonight, just hoping you don't share your bed with an unwelcome critter. After dark you notice glowing lights in the sky to your north. It has to be a city. At sunrise you'll start off in that direction.

Turn the page.

As soon as the sky lightens, you head off toward the lights. You've got one bottle of water left. Walking in the early morning is wise, since the daytime heat will sap your body of energy and moisture. You remember to breathe through your nose. Your body will lose less moisture that way.

Early on you make good progress. The ground here is mostly rocky, covered by dry brush. You see a few signs of animal life—some beetles, a spider, and a few scorpions. You're hungry, but not hungry enough to try eating any of the creatures.

Around noon you spot what looks like a rough road. It's the first sign of civilization you've seen! Excitedly, you pick up your pace and begin to follow the road. But the sun is getting stronger by the minute, and the heat is intense.

You're worried about heatstroke. Your body will begin shutting down if it gets too hot.

On one side of the road is a ridge with a large rock overhang. The shade there would offer a welcome rest, but can you afford to stop?

To continue on the road, turn to page 26.

To take shelter in the shade until evening, turn to page 32.

You could walk for miles and not find a better spot to climb. You tighten the straps on your backpack and start climbing.

You make good progress at first. The rock is loose, but you slowly work your way up. Soon you come to a much steeper rock face. It offers plenty of good handholds and footholds. You've always been a good climber, so you don't hesitate. You grab a handhold and start the climb. Before long, you've passed the hard part. Now you're scrambling up the remaining slope on all fours. It's still steep, but much easier.

You reach out to grab a rock that juts up, intending to use it to pull yourself up. "Ouch!" you yelp. A huge scorpion darts out from behind the rock. You pull your hand back, but it's too late. You've just been stung by one of the deadliest scorpions—the fat-tailed scorpion. You'll need to get treatment right away. As you look around, you realize that isn't likely to happen.

You keep moving. But after just a few minutes, the venom starts to move through your veins. Breathing gets more and more difficult. Your vision blurs as you collapse onto the desert floor.

Fat-tailed scorpion stings kill several people each year.

Turn to page **36.**

You're on the road to civilization, and you're not about to stop now. You continue on, fighting through the intense heat. Soon your pure water is gone. Your body is showing signs of dehydration. You need to either find water or rescue fast.

Off to one side, you see something shimmering in the distance. It looks like a big body of open water! But heading in that direction will take you away from the road.

To head for the shimmering area, go to page **27**.

To continue along the road, turn to page **34**.

Your head is aching and your thinking is slowing down. You know that means your body is desperately dehydrated. If there's a chance of finding water, you have to take it.

You stumble off the road. You walk and walk, but never seem to get any closer to the bright, shimmering pool. Dimly, you realize that you're chasing a mirage—a trick of heat and light that only looks like water. You've made a mistake. You have to get back to the road.

You turn around and start to head back, but soon you can't remember which direction is which. As you shuffle along, you trip over a rock and fall hard, turning your ankle badly in the process. You try to stand, but the pain is too great. Finally, you just lie there, panting. You know your body is beginning to shut down.

Turn the page.

Urine contains some body wastes, but it's still mostly water. The problem is that it's very salty— almost like drinking ocean water. If the urine is not concentrated, it's not as bad for you. You've been walking in the hot sun without drinking, though, which makes your urine concentrated. But it might be worth the risk.

You step away from camp and urinate into the bottle. You stand there for a moment, looking at the half-filled bottle. You know that if you look at it too long, you'll lose your nerve. You tip the bottle back and take a drink.

The warm urine tastes about as bad as you expected. You almost choke it back up, but force yourself to swallow.

There's not much more you can do but wait for rescuers. You lie down in a shady spot, but the desert heat is still intense. You're sweating.

Late that afternoon you notice that you're not sweating anymore. At first you think that's good news—it must not be as hot. But the sun is still beating down with incredible strength. Your body has run out of water with which to cool itself.

With no sweat, your body temperature begins to rise. Your skin turns red. You're dizzy and you have a headache. You try to urinate again in a desperate attempt for more liquid, but you can't go. Strangely, you don't really care. In the back of your mind, you know that these are all signs of severe dehydration.

As the sun sets, you close your eyes and drift off to sleep. Some part of you realizes that you won't wake up again.

THE END

To follow another path, turn to page 11.
To read the conclusion, turn to page 101.

Wave your arms or lie down with your hands and legs spread wide so a pilot will see you.

You're not desperate enough to drink your own urine. Urine is saltier than ocean water, and you know that drinking ocean water is deadly. You urinate near a dried bush. Your urine quickly disappears into the rocky, sandy soil.

Day turns into evening. You start to eat the potato chips, but the salt just makes you thirstier. You toss the rest aside, knowing that it's better to be hungry than it is to be thirsty.

By the following day, you are extremely dehydrated. You know you're in trouble when, despite the heat, you stop sweating. That means your body doesn't have any water to spare. You'll be lucky to survive another day.

But that evening you see lights in the sky. With them comes a low humming sound. It's a helicopter! Rescuers have found you! You wave your arms, screaming at the top of your lungs. By staying put and doing what you had to do to stay alive, you've survived your ordeal in the deadly Sahara.

THE END

To follow another path, turn to page 11.
To read the conclusion, turn to page 101.

Continuing to walk in this heat could be deadly. You carefully inspect the area. Finding no dangerous wildlife, you plop onto the ground, enjoying the precious shade. You finish the last of your pure water.

After several hours, the temperature begins to dip. The sun is lower in the sky and not nearly as strong. It's time to move.

You walk for an hour or two when you hear noises ahead. As you come over a small hill, you see people! It's a group of nomads, complete with tents and camels.

You hurry into the small camp. "Help!" you shout, falling to your knees. The surprised nomads yell something back at you, but you can't understand each other.

You grasp your throat and say, "Water, please!" A small boy rushes up with a container of water. As you gulp it, you use gestures to explain the plane crash. You mime using a phone, and they nod in understanding. It seems that they're promising to take you to a phone.

You've made it! Keeping your wits about you has allowed you to escape the deadly Sahara with your life.

THE END

To follow another path, turn to page 11.
To read the conclusion, turn to page 101.

Some desert nomads travel by camel.

Something doesn't seem quite right. What would a huge body of water be doing in the middle of the Sahara Desert? You squint at it and realize that it must be a mirage—a trick of heat and light that only looks like water. There's no help here. All you can do is continue. After about an hour, you collapse onto the ground. Without water, your body is shutting down. Your head aches and your thoughts are slow and confused. Your skin is flushed. You just can't go any longer.

As evening comes, you're drifting in and out of consciousness. You're only dimly aware when a small caravan of nomads spots you. You don't understand them as they try to talk to you, but that doesn't matter. You're still in a daze as they give you water, food, and shelter. The next day they take you to a village, where you can call for help.

A rescue helicopter comes for you and takes you to a hospital in Cairo. Your body has taken a beating. The dehydration has damaged your liver. But you're alive, and you'll heal. You're thankful—you know that even with good decisions, you needed plenty of luck to get out alive. You just wish the others on the plane with you had shared that luck.

THE END

To follow another path, turn to page 11.
To read the conclusion, turn to page 101.

Giving up is the worst thing you can do in the desert.

The pain is unbearable. It's hard to even think straight. You lie there, struggling, knowing that you're in deep trouble. Your mind slips in and out of consciousness.

You wake after dark, shivering. Your breath is coming in short, shallow gasps. Your mouth feels as if it's full of cotton. Your body is fighting with everything it has, but it's not enough. You need water and medical care immediately, and you're not going to get either.

You stare up at the night sky to see the stars, and then close your eyes for the last time.

THE END

To follow another path, turn to page 11.
To read the conclusion, turn to page 101.

The Sonoran Desert covers parts of Mexico, Arizona, and California.

CHAPTER 3

Lost in the Sonoran

It's late afternoon in the Sonoran Desert of northwestern Mexico. What started out as a fun hiking trip with your friends Alex, Jen, and Ruby has turned into a nightmare. While your friends stopped to rest, you decided to take a short hike by yourself. Now you're lost.

You haven't seen the trail for hours. You're alone, with only a small backpack containing a water canteen, a lighter, a pocketknife, your cell phone, and your journal. You left all of your food and other supplies with your friends. Your cell phone isn't getting a signal, and it doesn't seem as if help is coming any time soon.

Turn the page.

Rainstorms in the Sonoran are unpredictable.

The only good news you see is dark clouds in the distance. The clouds look as if they could bring rain. That would be a real stroke of luck. Rain would give you a chance to fill your canteen with pure, fresh water. But the storm could easily fizzle out before it gets here. Or it could veer in another direction.

There are only a couple of hours before the sun sets, and you're losing hope that you'll find your friends. Although the late afternoon temperature has to be over 90 degrees Fahrenheit, you know that the desert will cool down quickly, especially if a storm rolls through. You have plenty of time to find a place to camp for the night. But the idea of sleeping alone in the desert isn't very inviting.

Turn the page.

You're at a low altitude, but the landscape is dotted with rocky hills and mountains. If you could get to higher ground, maybe you'd be able to get a cell phone signal. If not, the view from up high might give you a clue of which direction to go for help.

To search for a place to camp for the night, go to page 43.

To head for higher ground, turn to page 44.

You don't want to spend a night without shelter, especially in the rain. If you conserve your water, you'll be fine until tomorrow. You have no food, but that's a minor concern. The body can go a long time without food. Water and shelter are your top priorities right now.

To one side a series of narrow canyons dips down below a plateau. The canyon walls would provide some shelter. But should you camp where you're not likely to be spotted? To your other side, the landscape rises gently toward a high ridge. You won't find much shelter there, but even a small campfire might be visible for miles.

To head for the canyons, turn to page **46.**

To camp on the higher, flatter ground, turn to page **49.**

There's often no cell phone reception in the desert.

You head off in the direction of a long ridge. The climbing isn't difficult. The slope is fairly gentle in most places. You're a good enough climber to handle the tougher spots. Within about an hour, you're standing on top of the ridge.

Your luck ends there, though. Your cell phone still isn't getting a signal. You try to figure out a direction to travel but can't see much. You shout at the top of your lungs, hoping your friends can hear you.

With a sigh, you begin the climb back down. You have just enough time and daylight to get back to flat ground. You can't see well enough to build a camp and collect fuel for a fire. A night spent shivering doesn't sound like much fun. You could keep walking. Staying on the move would keep you warm. But in the dark, you run the risk of falling or stepping on a rattlesnake.

To continue hiking, turn to page 51.

To try to sleep here, turn to page 56.

You head toward the series of canyons, grabbing dried brush along the way for a fire. The walls of the canyon will provide a perfect natural shelter.

You find a place to climb down into the deep, narrow canyon. You'll never be spotted here, but the odds of anyone searching for you tonight are low. Even if your friends call for help, the search probably won't start until tomorrow.

The canyon floor was carved by rushing water. Loose rock litters the floor. But finally you find a suitable camp. By sunset you have a small fire going. In the distance you hear the rumble of thunder. A light rain begins to fall. A look at the sky tells you that the heaviest rain is falling to the north, on higher ground. But after awhile a small trickle of water is running down the canyon wall. You easily fill your canteen, drink deeply, and then fill it again.

Steep canyons can flood in a short time.

Turn the page.

As you watch the water trickling in, you realize that a canyon may not be the safest place to be. Heavy rain could run off quickly and cause a flash flood. But the rain here is light—not even enough to put out your little fire. To abandon your camp now would mean climbing the canyon wall in near darkness.

To abandon your camp, turn to page **54**.

To remain here, turn to page **60**.

Taking shelter in the canyon is tempting, but it's too dangerous. With storm clouds on the horizon, there's a good chance of rain. In the desert even a little rain can quickly run downhill and create a flash flood.

You settle down on a flat, rocky spot. You won't have shelter, so starting a campfire is especially important. It will keep you warm, and it's possible that someone will spot its light.

You begin gathering desert brush. It feels dry and a bit brittle. You know it will burn easily. You also manage to find the dead husk of a small cactus. This will burn more slowly than the brush and should help keep a small fire going all night. As you're carefully dragging the cactus back to your camp, you hear a sound that no desert hiker wants to hear. It's the rattle of a venomous rattlesnake!

Turn the page.

The rattler is nestled in rocks only a few feet from you. Its body is coiled, with its head and rattles raised in the air. You know the rattle is a warning. If you move away slowly, you should be OK. But you also know that rattlesnakes are almost all meat. You haven't had much to eat today, and your stomach is growling. If you could kill the snake, you'd have the energy you'll need to hike to safety tomorrow.

To slowly back away and return to camp, turn to page **52**.

To try to kill the snake for its meat, turn to page **57**.

With no camp and no fire, you'll be freezing by morning. You decide to keep moving. Walking at night has its advantages. You won't sweat as much, which will conserve your body's water. As you walk, you finish what little water remains in your canteen. You've heard stories of people in the desert dying of dehydration despite still having some water. Conserving water is pointless when your body needs it now.

By dawn you're exhausted. You're more lost than ever, and now you're out of water. Nothing looks familiar. The only sign of civilization you've found is a rusted old motorcycle alongside a small canyon. As you look at the rusty machine, you have an idea. The motorcycle still has tires on it, and burning rubber creates a lot of smoke. You could build a signal fire. The only question out here is whether anyone would see it.

To continue walking, turn to page 65.

To try to build a signal fire, turn to page 67.

You may be hungry, but you're no fool. Picking a fight with an angry rattler is a bad idea. Slowly you back away from the snake. When you're at a safe distance, you turn and dart back to camp.

You use your lighter and a few wadded-up sheets of paper from your journal to get the fire going. Soon you've got a warm little blaze. As the sun sets, you watch the storm approach to the north. You get only a few drops here—not enough even to collect. It looks as if you'd been a few miles north, you'd have gotten a good soaking.

It's a restless night. You have to constantly feed the fire to keep it going. But at least you're warm and safe. At dawn you know it's time to move. It's best to do your walking before the midday heat.

Soon you're out of water and still have no idea where to go. The only sign of civilization you see is an old, abandoned motorcycle. The rusty bike looks like it's been sitting here for years.

The motorcycle does have its tires. You know that tires create a lot of smoke as they burn. They might make a good signal fire. But you're not sure you want to take the time to start a fire.

To continue walking, turn to page 65.

To try to build a signal fire, turn to page 67.

Canyon walls are often steep and treacherous.

You need to get out of the canyon now. Flash

floods can be sudden and violent, and you don't want to be trapped here.

You try to backtrack and find the spot where you climbed down. But in the dark, you don't recognize anything. You pick a spot that seems gentle, groping the canyon walls for footholds and handholds.

Slowly you work your way up the face of the canyon. You know that a fall now will be deadly. But luck is on your side. Soon the canyon wall begins to flatten out. On all fours, you scramble up out of the canyon and onto flat land. Your hands are shaking as you let out a huge sigh of relief.

Of course, now it's dark. You have nowhere to camp and no way to gather materials for a fire. It's going to be a cold, lonely night.

Turn the page.

You pick a spot on the desert floor and flop down. You curl up to conserve your body heat. A light mist falls from the sky, leaving your clothes damp and making the cold that much worse. You're shivering within an hour. Your body is losing heat quickly, starting to enter a state of hypothermia.

By the time dawn comes, you're almost paralyzed by the cold. All you want to do is stay and wait for the sun to warm you. But it will be several hours before the day really begins to heat up. You should get up and move around, but you're not sure you have the energy.

To get up and start moving, turn to page 62.

To remain here, waiting for the sun to warm you, turn to page 64.

You've seen survival TV shows where people catch snakes for food. All you have to do is grab the snake behind its head and then chop off the head.

You grab your pocketknife. You'll have to move fast. As you step forward, the snake uncoils and strikes. Quickly you step back out of its range. You dart to one side and stomp your foot down on the front half of the snake's body. You try to drive the tip of the knife through its skull, but in your hurry, you miss. A sharp pain burns through your hand and wrist. You've been bitten!

A rattlesnake's rattles are made of keratin—the same substance as human fingernails.

Turn the page.

You step back, stunned. The snake quickly slithers away. You know that rattlesnake bites are rarely fatal, but that's partly because people can get treatment. That's not an option for you. Under normal circumstances, you would probably be OK even without treatment. But your body is already weak from the heat, hunger, and dehydration.

You stumble back to camp and lie down. Your hand is swelling. You're entering a state of shock. You close your eyes, suddenly exhausted. You don't even have enough energy to build a fire.

By midnight, you're shivering. All the heat of the day is lost, and now your body is dealing with hypothermia. You're losing heat more quickly than your body can produce it. Your throat is dry and sore. Your hand feels as if it's on fire. You can't concentrate.

The next morning, the sun rises, but you never see it. It's only a matter of time until rescuers come, but it will be too late for you.

THE END

To follow another path, turn to page 11.
To read the conclusion, turn to page 101.

The heavy rain is miles away. You decide you'll be fine here. You lie down against a canyon wall, near your little fire. Soon you drift off to sleep.

You don't know how long you've slept, but you awaken with a shock. You're wet! A few inches of water is rushing along the canyon floor. Your fire has died, and it's very dark. You leap to your feet. The torrent of water is quickly up to your ankles, and then to your shins. It flows with surprising force.

You begin to panic—there's no way out! The sound of rushing water grows louder. It's up to your knees. The force of the current is already threatening to knock you off your feet. You cling to the canyon wall, but the water just keeps coming. Soon you can't hold on any longer. You shout at the top of your lungs as the current rips you away, but no one can hear you. Too late you realize that in the desert, flash floods can come from rain that falls miles away, especially in low-lying areas.

In the desert, a small creek can quickly become a rushing river.

As the water carries you, your head smashes into a rock. You're groggy and disoriented. Your head goes under. You gasp for breath, and water fills your lungs. You're horrified as you realize that you're about to drown in the middle of a desert.

THE END

To follow another path, turn to page 11.
To read the conclusion, turn to page 101.

With a groan, you pull yourself to your feet. You start walking, hoping that you'll find help.

As the sun climbs higher in the sky, the air grows warmer. You're still cold, but it's getting better. By noon, you're hot. Your water is gone, and your body has stopped sweating. You find a tiny pool of water—only a few sips—and slurp it greedily.

You come upon a narrow dirt road. Your heart races, knowing that you must be getting closer to civilization. About an hour later, you see a cloud of dust approaching. It's a truck. You wave your arms frantically as it approaches. You're filled with joy as it stops.

"Medico, por favor!" you shout. It means, "Doctor, please!" Your Spanish isn't great, but that message is more than clear.

The driver jumps out of the truck and helps you into the passenger seat. Soon you're bouncing down the road with a jug of precious water in hand, headed back to civilization.

It was a close call, but you've made it. You're going to be all right.

THE END

To follow another path, turn to page 11.
To read the conclusion, turn to page 101.

You're so cold that you just want to stay here a little longer. But an hour later, you're even colder. Your skin is pale. You begin to forget where you are and what you're doing. And when your mind clears, it's almost as if you don't care.

A part of your mind knows that these are all symptoms of advanced hypothermia. Your body is losing heat faster than it can replace it.

In time the sun gains strength and begins to warm you. But it is too late. Your body is shutting down, both from hypothermia and dehydration. You know that a rescue party will eventually find you here. But it will be too late. You'll soon be a victim of the harsh Sonoran Desert.

THE END

To follow another path, turn to page 11.
To read the conclusion, turn to page 101.

The large saguaro cactus is native to the Sonoran Desert.

You're miles from civilization. Even a good signal fire might be pointless. You decide that if you're getting out of this desert alive, it'll be on your own two feet.

As the sun climbs higher in the sky, the temperature soars. You breathe through your nose as you move, trying to conserve what little moisture remains in your mouth. At one point you use your pocketknife to cut open a cactus to get at the water inside. But all you succeed in doing is cutting up your hands and getting very little water in return.

Turn the page.

By noon you're starting to feel the effects of severe dehydration. Your body has stopped producing sweat, causing it to overheat. Your mind is getting fuzzy. Making decisions is becoming hard. Soon you just plop down against a rock. Just for a few minutes, you tell yourself. But the desert sun keeps beating down on you. You start fading in and out of consciousness. You realize that you're never going to get up. Your body is so starved for moisture that you can't even shed a tear for yourself.

THE END

To follow another path, turn to page 11.
To read the conclusion, turn to page 101.

A signal fire is one of the best ways to alert rescuers.

You're tired and quickly becoming dehydrated. You won't last much longer. It's time to send a signal. Your friends must have reported you missing by now. People will be looking for you.

You pull the old tires off the motorcycle. You start by building a small fire with pages from your journal and a big pile of dry desert brush. Once it's hot, you carefully arrange the tires on top of it.

Turn the page.

As the tires catch fire, they release huge plumes of thick, black smoke. The smoke rises up into the clear desert sky. You sit down in the patch of shade provided by a large rock. If this doesn't work, you know you're in deep trouble.

But your fire does work. After an hour or so, you hear a deep thump-thump-thump. You look in the sky and see a rescue helicopter. You lie flat on your back and spread your arms and legs wide. That way the pilot is more likely to see you. She does!

As the helicopter lands several yards away, you sigh with relief. You've kept your wits and managed to escape the desert with your life.

THE END

To follow another path, turn to page 11.
To read the conclusion, turn to page 101.

Helicopters are used for rescues because they don't need a runway to land.

Dry lake beds cover parts of Asia's vast Gobi Desert.

Alone in the Gobi

Your heart sinks as your dirt bike sputters and dies. This isn't good. You're alone in the middle of Asia's enormous Gobi Desert. You're spending the summer here with your parents while they study the region's ecology and wildlife. Riding the dirt bike is your favorite pastime. You're supposed to tell your parents if you travel more than a mile or two from your camp, but some days you forget. This is one of those days.

You've been riding the bike along the region's many dry, salt-covered lake beds. A quick guess tells you that you're at least 20 miles from camp. Nobody knows that you're here. They won't miss you until sunset, which is several hours from now.

The Gobi's sand dunes are popular with dirt bike riders.

You have no water or food. The dirt bike's saddlebag contains only a few items—emergency matches, a pocketknife, a roll of plastic food wrap, and some trash from a long-ago meal. What's worse is you don't know exactly how to get back to camp. Your motorcycle has a GPS that usually gets you home, but the bike's battery is dead. With no power, the GPS is useless.

Your options are limited. You could set out on foot, hoping you're going in the right direction. Or you could camp here, knowing that your parents will launch a rescue effort as soon as they realize you're missing.

To start walking in hopes of finding your way back to camp, turn to page **74**.

To camp here and prepare a fire for the night, turn to page **76**.

You gather your supplies and strike out. Even though the Gobi is a cool desert, the summer sun is warm. You figure that you can cover 20 miles in five or six hours. The only question is whether you're going the right way.

The desert is filled with rocks and dried lake beds. You spot a few small saxaul trees and small bits of dry brush, but little else.

If you find a trail in the Gobi, it's best to follow it.

After an hour of walking, you come across what looks like a trail. Animals have beaten down the ground here. You believe it's a caravan trail. Many of the Gobi's people are nomads. They use camels to move through the desert. If this is a trail, it might lead to help. But the trail heads off in a different direction. You don't think it's the way back to your parents' camp.

To follow the trail, turn to page 77.

To ignore the trail and continue looking for your parents, turn to page 78.

By tomorrow your parents will be looking for you. All you have to do is stay alive until they find you. Walking into the desert alone, with few supplies, probably isn't the best way to do that. You'll camp here and wait for rescue.

Nearby are several large boulders. It's the perfect spot. If you camp there and build a small fire, the boulders will trap some of the heat and keep you warm. But gathering fuel for the fire will take a long time—there's not a lot to burn out here. Maybe that time would be better spent searching for water. Without water, you won't last long.

To search for water, turn to page 79.

To work on building a fire, turn to page 80.

This trail is the first sign of civilization you've seen so far, and you're not about to leave it. You choose a direction and start off. Maybe you'll find a small settlement somewhere. Or maybe a group of nomads will come along.

After two hours the trail remains deserted. Did you make a mistake? You're sure now that you're heading in a direction away from your parents' camp. Every step you take will make you that much harder to find. The sun will set in an hour or so. You could continue on the trail through the night. Or you could climb a nearby ridge to see if you can spot your parents' camp from above.

To try climbing for a better view of your surroundings, turn to page 92.

To stick to the trail, turn to page 94.

You're sure the trail leads away from your parents' camp. So you continue the way you were headed. Another hour passes. Nothing looks familiar. You're getting thirstier. And the sun is sinking low in the sky.

A tall ridge is ahead. From the top of the ridge, you might be able to see some sign of civilization. But it looks like a dangerous climb, and there isn't much daylight left. It might be safer just to camp here for the night.

To camp, turn to page **80.**

To climb the ridge, turn to page **92.**

Water is your top priority. Without it, you won't last more than a couple of days. But where can you find water in the middle of a desert?

You scan the landscape. The soil is loose and dry. In the distance you see a thick bunch of vegetation along low-lying land. Plants usually grow where there's a water supply.

Another option is to build a solar still. Your dirt bike's saddlebag holds everything you need to build one—a soda can and a roll of plastic wrap that you use to wrap sandwiches. But you have never built a solar still before. You're not positive it will work.

To work on a solar still, turn to page 82.

To dig for water, turn to page 86.

The Gobi gets very cold at night. You'll
need a fire to keep warm. As long as you conserve
energy and your body's water, you'll be fine
until tomorrow.

You set out to gather fuel. You find a patch
of small saxaul trees. You break off several of the
small branches. You also peel off some bark from
the tree's trunk. There's moisture behind the bark,
and you lap it up. It's not much, but you're happy
for any drop of water you can find.

Soon you have a nice pile of fuel for your fire.
You keep the fire small. You don't want to run out
of fuel too soon.

As your fire burns, you decide to get one more
load of fuel. You find a bunch of small, dry brush
and begin pulling it up. But suddenly, you notice
something that makes you freeze in place. It's a
snake—a central Asian pit viper! It's one of the
deadliest snakes in the world.

Saxaul shrubs and trees are plentiful in the Gobi Desert.

To slowly back away and return to your fire,
turn to page 85.

To try to chase the snake away with a stick,
turn to page 89.

Digging for water could be a lot of work with no reward. You'll try your luck with a solar still. You start by digging a hole a few feet deep. It's not hard to do in the dry, loose soil. You find a sharp rock and make cuts in the top of the soda can. You then rip off the top, forming a cup.

Next you need to add moisture to the bottom of the still. Your dirt bike's radiator contains water for cooling the engine. The water could be tainted, so drinking it directly is a bad idea.

Instead you disconnect the radiator and dump the water into the hole you've dug. Then you place

your cup at the bottom and cover the hole with the plastic wrap. You weight down the plastic with rocks so it doesn't blow away. You add one small rock to the middle, creating a small dip. Water will drip down to the dip and then into the cup. You finish the job and cross your fingers.

Solar Still

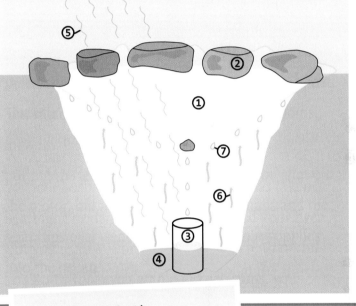

1. transparent plastic

2. stones to hold plastic in place

3. container to catch fresh water

4. non-drinkable liquid

5. sunlight

6. evaporation

7. condensation dripping from the bottom of the plastic

Turn the page.

It's time to gather materials to burn. There's not much available out here. It's going to be a pretty pathetic campfire.

Around sunset you check the still. It's working! A small sip of pure, clean water has collected in the cup. It's really not much water, but it feels like a major victory.

It's a long, cold night. Your fire goes out before dawn. But you're alive.

Turn to page **97**.

You know that if you leave the snake alone, it will most likely leave you alone. You back away very slowly, taking care not to startle the viper. It watches you closely and then quickly slithers away in the opposite direction.

With a deep sigh of relief, you return to your camp. You tend your little fire, which keeps you warm for most of the night. You're hungry, thirsty, and uncomfortable, but all things considered, you're doing quite well. After what seems like forever, you see light on the horizon. The sun is finally rising.

Turn to page **97.**

Nighttime temperatures in the Gobi can drop below freezing, even in summer.

There's a good chance you can find water if you dig in a low-lying area. You head down into the small depression and get to work. At first it's easy. But as you dig deeper, the ground becomes firmer. You have to work harder.

You're breathing heavily from the effort. Your body is dripping with sweat. "Just a little deeper," you tell yourself. But after almost an hour of hard digging, the ground is still bone dry.

You step back, wiping the sweat from your brow. You notice your hands are shaking. You've made a terrible mistake. All that hard work has used much of your body's water reserve. Now your clothing is soaked in sweat, and the sun is setting.

With no time or energy to build a fire, you huddle in a spot where two small boulders form a natural windbreak. But the temperature in the Gobi drops drastically after sunset. You shiver in your sweat-soaked clothing.

Your throat is dry and scratchy. You know you're suffering from early signs of both dehydration and hypothermia.

Turn the page.

It's a long and miserable night. At sunrise you know you should build a signal fire, but you don't have the energy. At one point late in the day, you see a trail of dust in the distance. It's a vehicle! You stand to run toward it, but as soon as you get up, you feel dizzy. Before you realize it, you're face down on the ground. You've fainted. With so little water, your heart is having a hard time pumping blood to your brain.

You've banged your head against a sharp rock. Everything is fuzzy, and your head is bleeding. The vehicle is gone. The driver never saw you.

You fall to the ground. You lie there exhausted, dehydrated, and bleeding. You'll do all you can do to stay alive, but your body's resources are almost spent. The desert has beaten you, and you've probably just missed your only hope of rescue.

THE END

To follow another path, turn to page 11.
To read the conclusion, turn to page 101.

You've found fuel here, and you don't want to give it up. You grab a long, solid piece of brush and wave it at the snake.

But the snake doesn't turn away. Instead, it flattens its body and begins shaking its tail. You shout at the snake and swipe at it with your stick again. But you've forgotten something important. The central Asian pit viper is an aggressive snake. It was warning you to back away. In the blink of an eye, the snake strikes. You've been bitten in the leg! You yelp in pain and run back to your fire.

You soon feel the effects of the venom. Your vision blurs, and you begin to see double. You're sluggish, and every muscle in your body hurts. You lie down and groan in pain. The snake's bite isn't usually fatal, but in this situation, it's big trouble. Your body is without food and water. Your natural defenses are weakened.

Turn the page.

The central Asian pit viper's venom causes pain and muscle paralysis.

You stop tending your fire, and it burns out. That leaves you shivering as the night grows colder and colder.

By morning you can't even get up. Everything hurts. You lie there, waiting for rescue. But you're lying against a boulder, largely hidden from view. You don't have a signal fire to tell rescuers where you are. Meanwhile, your body is losing more and more precious moisture. Soon you're fading in and out of consciousness. Late that afternoon, you lose consciousness for the last time. Your desert adventure is over.

THE END

To follow another path, turn to page 11.
To read the conclusion, turn to page 101.

You're a good climber, so a little ridge doesn't scare you. At first the climbing is easy. But soon the ridge grows steeper. Several times rock breaks away under your hands or feet. You have to scramble to keep from tumbling down the slope.

The climbing makes you sweat. You know your body is using up precious water. But if you can find your destination from up here, it will all be worth it.

As you pull yourself up and scan the horizon, you almost shout with joy. It worked! Far off in the distance, you can see your parents' camp! You carefully make note of the direction, then start down the far side of the ridge.

You soon realize your mistake. This side of the ridge is very difficult to climb. And now the sun is setting, making it hard to see handholds and footholds. In one spot where the slope is almost a sheer drop, the rock crumbles beneath your feet.

Before you realize what's happening, you're falling! It's not a long fall, but as you crash into a rock ledge below, you lose consciousness. When you wake, it's dark. You groan with pain—both of your legs have been shattered in the fall. The bone in your right leg juts out through your jeans. The pain is so intense that you momentarily black out again.

Weakly, you shout for help. But you know that no one will hear you. And on the face of this ridge, there's almost no chance anyone will see you. You close your eyes, knowing your fate has been sealed.

THE END

To follow another path, turn to page 11.
To read the conclusion, turn to page 101.

It's tempting to climb, but staying here may be your best bet. You can walk through the night. That will keep you warm. If you don't find anything by tomorrow, you can build a signal fire.

You're shocked at how dark it is out here. You have only a sliver of moonlight to guide you. But as you squint and look ahead, you notice something. There's a flicker of light up ahead. It looks like firelight.

You move carefully, watching your step in the dark. There's definitely a fire ahead! Soon you hear voices as well. You've found a caravan! You can hardly believe your luck—this is one of the most sparsely populated areas in the world.

You shout out as you approach, not wanting to frighten the people. "Hello! I need help!"

The nomads look at you at first with suspicion. They don't speak English and probably aren't used to running into strangers out here. But soon they see the shape you're in.

Gobi nomads raise camels, along with horses, cattle, sheep, and goats.

Turn the page.

A man rushes out to you and takes you by the arm. He speaks, but you can't understand him any better than he understands you.

Still the nomads seem to understand your situation. They rush to bring you water and food—noodles and what you think is boiled mutton. You've heard that the local people are famous for their hospitality, and you see that it's true.

You still have a long way to go—you may have to find a town or village to call your parents. Your desert journey isn't over yet, but now you know that you'll be OK.

THE END

To follow another path, turn to page 11.
To read the conclusion, turn to page 101.

You've made the best of your situation so far, and today you're hoping all that work pays off. Now that the sun is up, you know your parents will be looking for you. You need to help them find you. You search for materials to burn. After a few hours, you have a sizable stack of vegetation. But most of it is dry. It won't produce much smoke.

Once again you look to your dirt bike for a resource. The bike's motor needs oil to run smoothly. And motor oil makes lots of black smoke when it burns. You drip the oil over the fuel you've gathered. You even soak some sand in gasoline. The fire lights quickly and sends up big plumes of smoke. The smoke rises. If your parents are anywhere nearby, they're bound to see it.

Turn the page.

Almost all roads in the Gobi Desert are rough and unpaved.

All you can do now is wait. Soon the fire starts to die down. It's giving off less and less smoke. You throw everything else you have onto it, knowing that this is your best shot. And it works. Within 10 minutes you see a trail of dust rising in the distance. It's your father's jeep!

"Dad!" you shout as you wave your arms. You've never been so happy to see him. You've survived your ordeal in the Gobi Desert. You can't wait to tell your friends about your adventure.

THE END

To follow another path, turn to page 11.
To read the conclusion, turn to page 101.

Desert oases provide food, shade, and water to travelers.

CHAPTER 5

Stay Alive

The desert can be a beautiful and fascinating place. But it's also full of danger. Extreme temperatures, dangerous wildlife, and lack of water can add up to disaster quickly. Time isn't on your side. Your body can go weeks without food, but you'll die in a matter of days without water. If you're sweating and working hard, you'll die even sooner.

Survival in the desert starts with your mind. You have to plan. You've got to collect what resources you have and use them effectively. If you've got water, don't just save it. Your body can go into a state of severe dehydration before you even realize it's happening. Many people in such situations have died with water still in their canteens. Stay hydrated!

Staying hydrated is the best thing you can do to survive the desert.

It's important that you remain calm. If you panic, you'll make bad decisions. You've also got to maintain the will to live. As soon as you give up hope, you're all but finished. Stay positive and focused on the goals at hand—staying alive and finding rescue.

Always be aware of your situation. Any time you go alone into the desert or other remote location, it's best to tell someone what you're doing and where you are going to be. If you've done that, it may be best to stay put. Find a spot with some shade. Avoid any activity that will make you sweat and lose precious water.

But if nobody knows where you are, you'll have to consider other options. Rescue isn't coming to you, so you'll have to go find it. You might signal for help with a fire, or you might have to take off in search of civilization.

Desert roads are usually not well-marked and may end without warning.

If that happens, look for roads. If you find one, stay close to it. Roads lead to people. And there's always the chance that someone will drive by.

Every decision you make in the desert can be the difference between life and death. Making the right choices isn't easy. Could you eat bugs, snakes, or scorpions? Could you use the materials around you to build shelter and fire? Could you stay positive and focused even when everything seems to go against you?

If you can answer "yes" to these questions, you might have what it takes to get out of a desert alive.

Real Survivors

Mauro Prosperi
In 1994 Mauro Prosperi was running in a race across the Sahara when a sand storm caused him to lose the trail. Prosperi had little water and no food. At one point he managed to catch two small bats. He killed the animals and drank their blood. He walked toward a mountain range until a small band of nomads spotted him and took him to a nearby village. Prosperi spent six days in the desert and lost 33 pounds. He survived, but extreme dehydration caused severe damage to his liver.

Aron Ralston
In 2003 Aron Ralston went alone into the Utah desert to hike and climb in its long system of canyons. But as he climbed, a large boulder fell, pinning his arm to the canyon wall. He couldn't move his arm or the

boulder. He was trapped in the canyon with little food or water for more than five days. Finally, he used a cheap pocketknife to cut off his own arm, freeing him from the boulder. Hungry, dehydrated, and bleeding, he hiked out of the canyon. With one arm, he managed to rappel down a cliff, where he found a small pool of water. He hiked back toward a road until he found a family of hikers, who called for help. Ralston wrote a book about his ordeal, which was later made into the movie *127 Hours*.

Henry Morello

In 2011 Henry Morello was driving home from a restaurant through the Arizona desert when he took a wrong turn. Morello, 84, got stuck in a ditch on a remote road. He was stranded for five days. His car battery and cell phone battery were dead. He took metal parts off of his car and placed them on the roof, hoping they'd reflect the sun's rays and be seen by rescuers. During the cold nights, he used his car's floor mats as blankets. He even drank windshield wiper fluid. Rescuers found him and rushed him to the hospital, where he recovered.

SURVIVAL QUIZ

1. What is your most important resource in the desert?

A. Food

B. Water

C. Shelter

D. Fuel for a fire

2. If you encounter a deadly snake, how should you deal with it?

A. Try to kill it for food

B. Wave your arms and scare it away

C. Back away slowly, making no sudden movements

D. Ignore it

3. Where do many dangerous desert snakes and scorpions make their homes?

A. In desert trees or shrubs

B. Deep in underground caves

C. On top of mountains

D. Under rocks

Answers: B, C, D

READ MORE

Borgenicht, David, and Justin Heimberg. *The Worst-Case Scenario Survival Handbook: Extreme Junior Edition.* San Francisco: Chronicle Books, 2008.

Doeden, Matt. *Trapped in a Canyon!: Aron Ralston's Story of Survival.* Mankato, Minn.: Capstone Press, 2007.

O'Shei, Tim. *The World's Most Amazing Survival Stories.* Mankato, Minn.: Capstone Press, 2007.

INTERNET SITES

Use FactHound to find Internet sites related to this book. All of the sites on FactHound have been researched by our staff.

Here's all you do:
Visit *www.facthound.com*
Type in this code: 9781429675437

GLOSSARY

dehydration (dee-hye-DRAY-shuhn)—a life-threatening medical condition caused by a lack of water

flash flood (FLASH FLUHD)—a sudden flood that comes with little warning, usually as the result of heavy rainfall

heatstroke (HEETSTROHK)—a life-threatening medical condition caused by prolonged heat exposure

hypothermia (hye-puh-THUR-mee-uh)—a condition that can occur when a person's body temperature drops several degrees below normal

mirage (muh-razh)—an illusion; in the desert, heat rising off of desert sand can appear to look like water, forming a mirage

nomad (NOH-mad)—a person who moves from place to place instead of living in one spot

saxaul tree (SAKS-awl TREE)—a tree or shrub that holds water in its bark; it is common in the Gobi Desert

venom (VEN-uhm)—a poison transmitted by the bite or sting of an animal

viper (VYE-pur)—a snake that kills its prey with venom

BIBLIOGRAPHY

Alloway, David. *Desert Survival Skills.* Austin: University of Texas Press, 2000.

Fears, J. Wayne. *The Complete Book of Outdoor Survival.* Iola, Wis.: Krause Publications, 1999.

Grubbs, Bruce. *Desert Hiking Tips: Expert Advice on Desert Hiking and Driving.* Helena, Mont.: Falcon Publishing, 1998.

Grylls, Bear. *Man vs. Wild: Survival Techniques From the Most Dangerous Places on Earth.* New York: Hyperion: 2008.

Lehman, Charles A. *Desert Survival Handbook: How to Prevent and Handle Emergency Situations.* Phoenix: Primer Publishers, 1998.

Stroud, Les. *Survive: Essential Skills and Tactics to Get out of Anywhere—Alive.* New York: Collins, 2008.

Towell, Colin. *The Survival Handbook: Essential Skills for Outdoor Adventure.* New York: DK, 2009.

Weigel, Marlene. *Encyclopedia of Biomes (Vol. 1).* Detroit: UXL, 2000.

INDEX